This Is the
CHURCH

by Sarah Raymond Cunningham

illustrated by
Ariel Landy

beaming books

MINNEAPOLIS

There's a little rhyme that children say,
a song they sing sometimes when they play.

This rhyme is about God's family.
To do it, just move your hands like me.

Here is the church, here is the steeple,
open the doors and see all the people

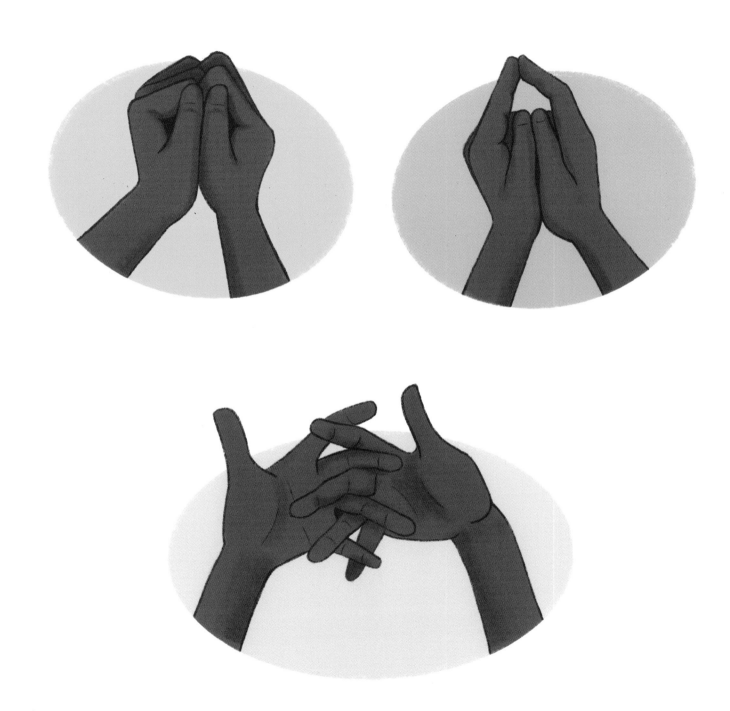

What a great rhyme! Isn't it neat?!
But wait—this story's not yet complete!

There's more to the church than just those two lines.
To learn about God's family, let's add to this rhyme!

Some churches are so big and wide,
ten thousand people can fit inside!

Other churches are really quite small.
They fit just a few people, and that is all!

Some people have church right where they are,
right in their houses. **That's not very far!**

And not all churches have roofs and floors.
Some don't have steeples, some don't have doors.

Some people have church under the stars,
and God comes and meets them right where they are.

And in places where it's not safe to be found,
some people even have church underground!

And church isn't something that stands still, you know.
The church follows God's people **wherever they go!**

The church moves in buses, planes, and cars.
To share God's love, the church has gone far.

The church works among the sick, hungry, and poor,
with people in need wherever they are.

It's gone to cities, it's gone to towns,
to school and to work—the church gets around!

But how does this work? How can this be?
Can a church really move like you and me?

That's the secret! It certainly can!
Church moves through your feet, it works through your hands.

The people ARE the church, don't you see?
Church is a word for God's family.

'Cause Jesus said, "Where there are two or three . . . who gather in my name, that's where I'll be."

So let's go back to the old rhyme now.
Get your hands ready, we'll show you how.

Here is a building,
it may have a steeple.

But where is the church?

The church is the people!

On this day, the church welcomes you.
You're part of God's people, you're the church too!

25 24 23 22 21 20   1 2 3 4 5 6 7 8

ISBN: 978-1-5064-4532-8

Library of Congress Cataloging-in-Publication Data
Names: Cunningham, Sarah Raymond, 1978- author. | Landy, Ariel,
    illustrator.
Title: This is the church / by Sarah Raymond Cunningham ; illustrated by
    Ariel Landy.
Description: Minneapolis : Beaming Books, 2020. | Audience: Ages 3-8 |
    Summary: "This picture book is about how the Christian church is the
    people that are a part of it; the story explores different "kinds" of
    churches, from traditional congregations that meet in buildings, to
    underground churches that are constantly moving. But ultimately, the
    church is the people, and people are meant to show God's love to others
    and grow in community with each other"-- Provided by publisher.
Identifiers: LCCN 2019031923 | ISBN 9781506445328 (hardcover)
Subjects: LCSH: Church--Juvenile literature.
Classification: LCC BV600.3 .C86 2020 | DDC 262--dc23
LC record available at https://lccn.loc.gov/2019031923

VN0004589; 9781506445328; DEC2019

Beaming Books
510 Marquette Avenue
Minneapolis, MN 55402
Beamingbooks.com